LET'S PLAY

a coloring and journaling book

created by terri st.cloud

Let's play!

Which, I'm thinking, means no rules.

Color with whatever you feel like.

inside or outside the lines.

Journal on one page,

let it roll over onto another if you want.

It's a coloring book,

It's a journal.

It's a place for you to be with you.

However works for you.

Ahhhh...

maybe trust
is the door
thru which
magic enters...

if you travel
around a planet-
if you land
on a distant
galaxy-
will anything
but love
get you there?

she would take
herself by the
shoulders
and turn her
face,
her heart,
her bones,
her entire being -
towards the sun.

magic showed up
again and again.
she learned
to look for it,
recognize it,
and delight in it!

and she valued herself...

_____
_____

_____
_____

_____

_____

_____

_____

_____
_____
_____
_____

Buried Treasure

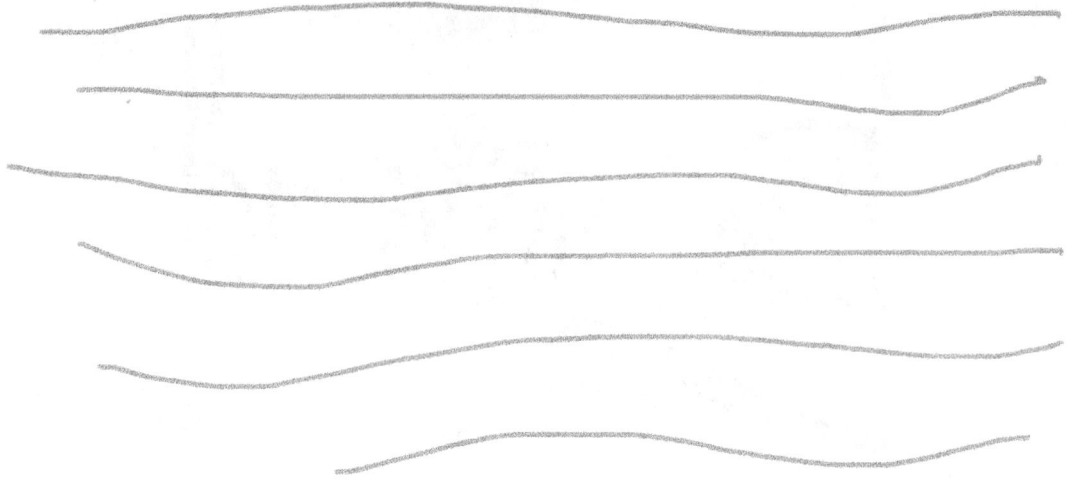

and she met
herself
for tea -

beyond words,
beyond thought,
all she could do
was feel it,
acknowledge it,
dance with it,
and understand
it was all
part of her
and she part of it...

_____
_____

_____

_____

_____

_____

_____

_____

touching
the sky
all day
would have
to make you
wise.

whatever
happens
let
it
happen
because
you
are
REAL.

like a flower
bending in the rain -
she'd get up
again
and again
and again.

always with me,
waiting inside.
sometimes quietly,
sometimes not.
it is when i stop
and listen
that i honor your
presence.
it is when i follow
what i hear
that i honor
my wholeness.

_____
_____
_____
_____
_____

what does the
key
to the sky
look like?

we are
each other's
candles...

dance
little girl
dance!
let the beat
of your heart
be your
rhythm.

she brought
it with her
from the stars.
and after she
spread some of
its light,
she would bring
it back.
because now
she knew.

_____
_____
_____
_____
_____
_____
_____

and she had hope...

wind
sings
thru
the
chimes
quieting
my
mind
helping
me
to
remember
to
just
be.

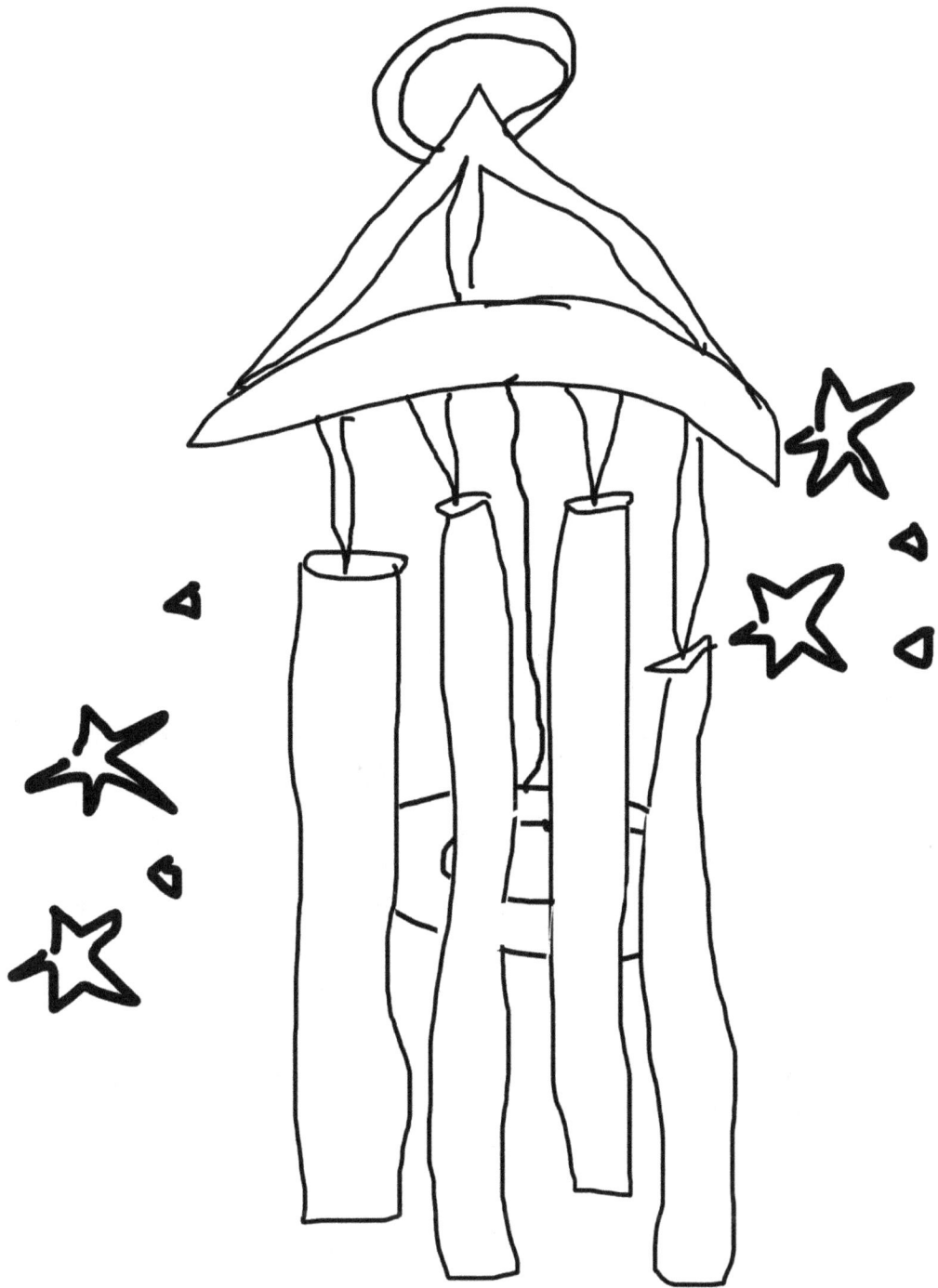

sometimes
when the wind's
just right,
i fold up my clothes
into a kite,
i hook up a ribbon
to my belt -
and go off
flying
all by myself.

if i could
teach you
anything
it would be
to hear your heart.
and to know
your beauty
and to believe
in your
possibilities.

and the door stood
waiting to be
opened.
self love now would
be the key.
reaching for the latch,
she closed her eyes,
held herself
with compassion
and pushed.

_____

_____

_____

_____

_____

_____

there they sat
around the table.
all ages.
from the little girl
to the old woman.
surrounded by
tea cups, cookies
and laughter.
love filling
their eyes
and the room.
sliding the chair
my way,
they invite me in.
'come we've been
waiting for you.'
sitting down
and joining them,
i begin to know myself.

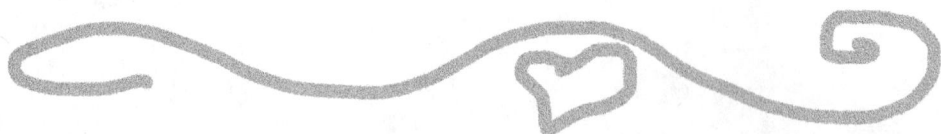

i am enough.

I AM Enough

I AM Enough

I AM Enough

I AM Enough

and she understood
how important
it is to be
mindful.

_____

_____

_____

_____

_____

_____

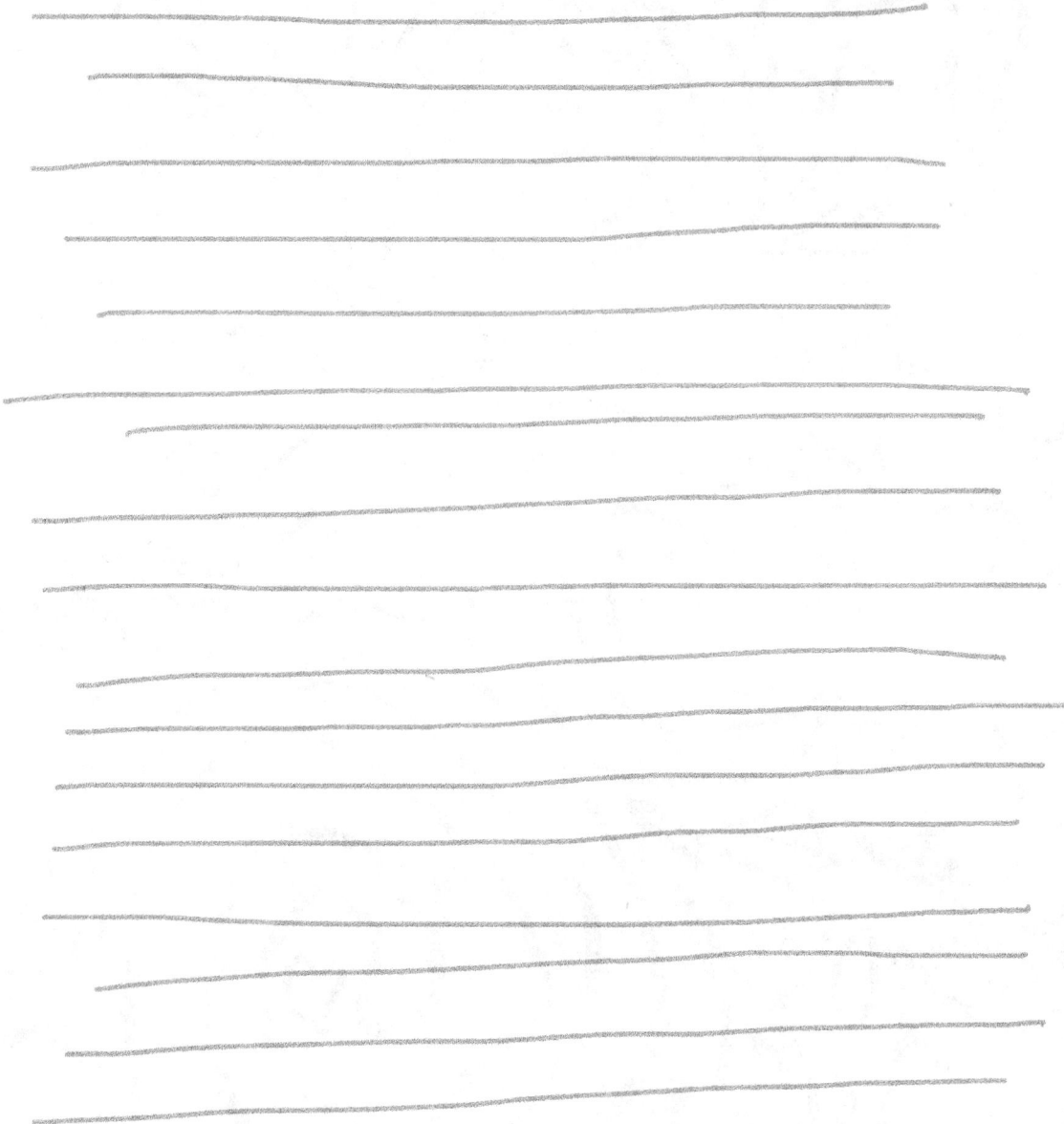

you are
stronger
than you know -

your inner voice
is the voice of
the soul...
follow it.

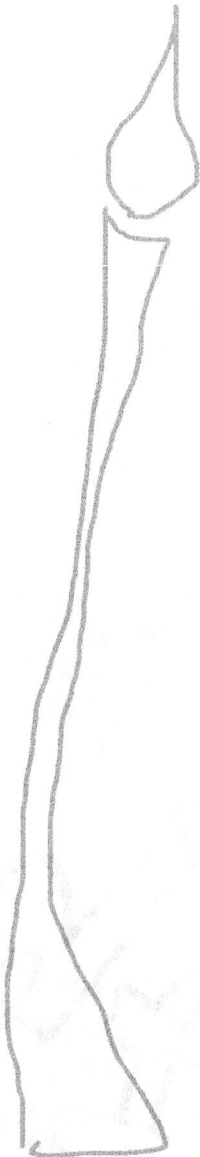

walking thru
the rain,
her tears joined
the raindrops.
pretty soon
there was nothing
left to do
but dry off
and have a cup
of tea.

believe

_____

_____

_____

_____

_____

_____

_____

_____

_____

BELIEVE

it was time
she remembered
she belonged
to the light.

she really was
a child of the
universe.
and the more
she played her way
to the depths
around her,
the more she
understood that.

it was time
to fly -

and she had love.
and she gave love.
and when she was
really really present
she was love.

i will not
allow myself
to be less than
i am
to meet
anybody's
expectations.

she turned
towards
the trust
and stopped
running.

TRUST

stepping
into her
life,
she felt
renewed
energy
and beamed!

unwrapping
her hands
from around
her heart -
she offered
her all...

honor
your
self.

_____
_____

_____
_____

bone
sigh
arts
.com

My name's terri st.cloud.

I like to call these pictures that

I draw 'st.cloudies.'

That makes me smile.

The pictures make me smile.

I hope they make you do the same.

You can find some of my other art -

the stuff I call 'bone sighs' -

on my website - www.BoneSighArts.com.

Thanks for playing with me!

www.ingramcontent.com/pod-product-compliance
Lightning Source LLC
Chambersburg PA
CBHW081141090426
42736CB00018B/3431